D0422176

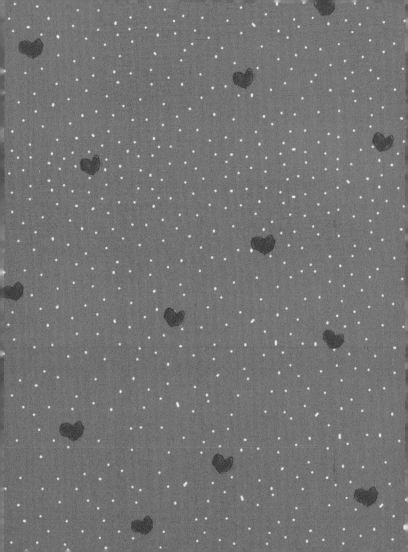

A gift for:

_____

From:

_____

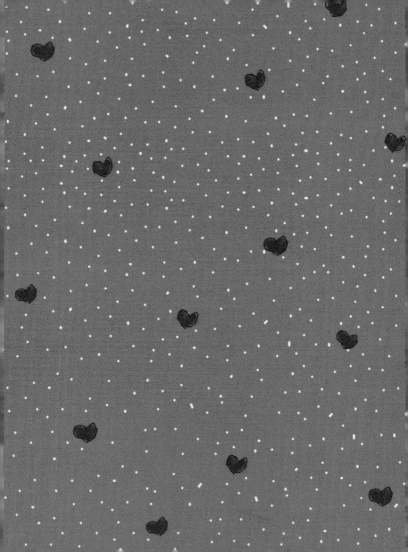

God Thinks You're
Wonderful,
Mom!

Illustrated by Chris Shea

Max Lucado

Published by
THOMAS NELSON™
Since 1798

www.thomasnelson.com

John and Alyssa DeLosSantos
because you love moms like God does.
—Max

To my mother
who always bought me crayons
and coloring books and said it was okay
to color outside the lines.
—Chris

Some things

only a mom can do.

Only a mother

can powder a baby's behind

with one hand

and hold the phone

with the other.

Only a mom can discern

which teen is entering the door

just by the sound of the

key in the lock.

Only a mom can spend a

day wiping noses,

laundering enough socks

for the Yankees,

balancing a checkbook down to $1.27,

and still mean it when she

thanks God for her kids.

Some things

only a mom can fix.

Like Hamburger Helper

without the hamburger.

Like the cabinet door

her husband couldn't and his

bruised ego when he

found out that she could.

Broken shoelace?

Broken heart?

Breaking out on your face?

Breaking up

with your sweetheart?

Moms can handle that.

Some things

only a mom can know.

The time it takes

to drive from piano lesson to

Little League practice?

She knows.

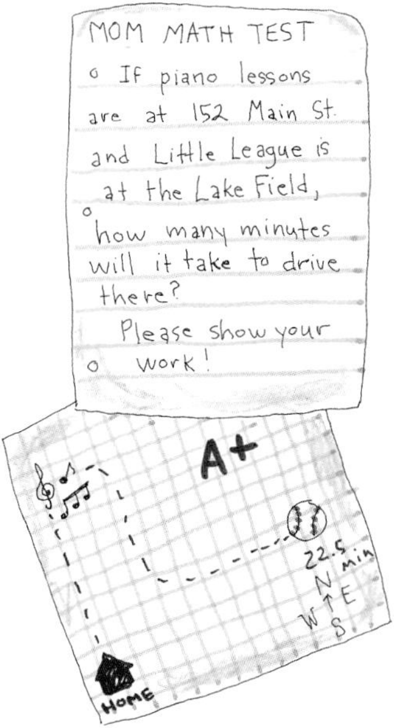
MOM MATH TEST
If piano lessons are at 152 Main St. and Little League is at the Lake Field, how many minutes will it take to drive there?
Please show your work!
A+
22.5 min
N
E
W
S
HOME

How many pizzas

you need for a middle

school sleepover?

Mom knows.

How many

Weight Watcher points are

left in the day and days are left

in the semester?

Mom knows.

Moms are a breed apart.

The rest of us can only wonder,

only ponder.

We can only ask,

"Mom, what's it like?"

When you felt the foot

within your womb,

when the infant cry first

filled the room . . .

to think that you

and heaven just circled

the moon . . .

What's that like?

And the day

the bus pulled to a stop and

you zipped the jacket up

to the top and placed a kiss on a

five-year-old's cheek . . .

and waved good-bye,

then saw the trike—

silent and still—

what's it like?

The first time you noticed

his voice was deep.

The first time she asked if

you were asleep and wanted to

know when love was real.

And you told her.

Thank you,
God . . .

How did you feel?

Then the candles were lit.

She came down the aisle.

Did you weep?

Did you smile?

MOM'S
JOURNAL
It seems
like only
yesterday
she was
a baby!!
I'm so
proud!!

And when

your child with child

told you the news, and in the quiet

of the corner asked for clues.

"Mom," she whispered,

"what's it like?"

What you told her would

you tell us?

Indeed, what's it like?

There's another thing we'd

like to know, Mom.

Did you know

that God loves you with

an everlasting love?

He has tattooed your name on

the palm of his hand.

"I have written your
name on my hand."

Isaiah 49:16

You are valuable to him...

not because of what you do

but simply because you are.

God, your thoughts are
precious to me. They are
so many! If I could count
them, they would be more
than all the grains of sand.

Psalm 139:17-18

His thoughts of you outnumber

the sand on the shore.

You never

leave his mind,

escape his sight,

flee his thoughts.

MEMO

If I rise with
the sun in the east
and settle in the west
beyond the sea,
even there you would
guide me.

Psalm 139:9-10

God cherishes you

like Stradivarious would

his newest violin.

He knows you better than

you know you and has

reached his verdict:

he loves you still.

You need not win his love.

You already have it.

And, since you can't win it,

you can't lose it.

How does

that make you feel?

– Hmmm…

God loves you simply because he

has chosen to do so.

He loves you.

Personally. Powerfully. Passionately.

He lives to hear your

heartbeat.

He loves to hear

your prayers.

...for all
my blessings...

"Give all your worries to him, because he cares about you."

I Peter 5:7

If something is important to you,

it's important to him.

He has never

taken his eyes off you.

— Not for a millisecond.

He's always near.

Time for
School !

He's as near to you on Monday

as on Sunday.

He will love you.

Always.

No matter what.

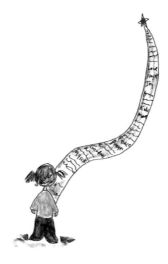

Our hearts

are not large enough to

contain the blessings that God

wants to give.

He made

galaxies no one has

ever seen and dug canyons

we have yet to find.

Beautiful!

He commands

whales to spout salty air,

petunias to

perfume the night,

— ммм

— ммм

— Lovely!

f f
f

and songbirds

to chirp joy into spring.

Above the earth,

flotillas of clouds endlessly shape

and reshape;

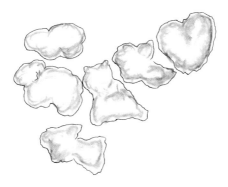

within the earth,

strata of groaning rocks

shift and turn.

His greatest gift?

He has chosen to give you

the gift of himself.

Sunsets steal our breath.

Caribbean blue stills

our hearts.

Newborn babies stir

our tears.

But take all these away—

strip away the sunsets,

oceans, and cooing babies—

and leave us in the Sahara,

and we still have reason to

dance in the sand.

Why?

Because God is with us.

We are never alone.

Ever.

God has said,

"I will never leave you;

I will never abandon you."

Hebrews 13:5

God loves you

too much to leave you alone,

so he hasn't.

So kick up your heels

for joy.

The greatest

discovery in the universe

is the greatest love in

the universe—

God's love.

He loves

each one of us like

there was only one of

us to love.

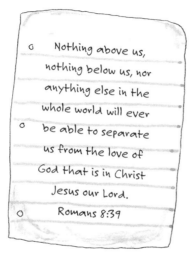

Nothing above us, nothing below us, nor anything else in the whole world will ever be able to separate us from the love of God that is in Christ Jesus our Lord.

Romans 8:39

Though

mind-numbingly mighty,

he comes in the soft of night

and touches us

with the tenderness of

an April snow.

He is the shepherd

who loves you.

So be kind to yourself.

God thinks

you're worth his kindness.

And he's a good judge

of character.

He thinks you're wonderful!

By the way, Mom.

I think you're wonderful, too!

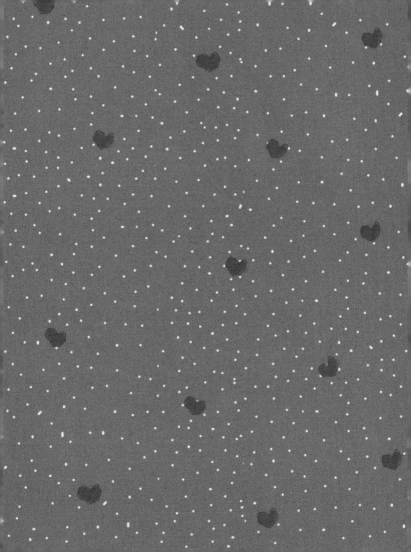

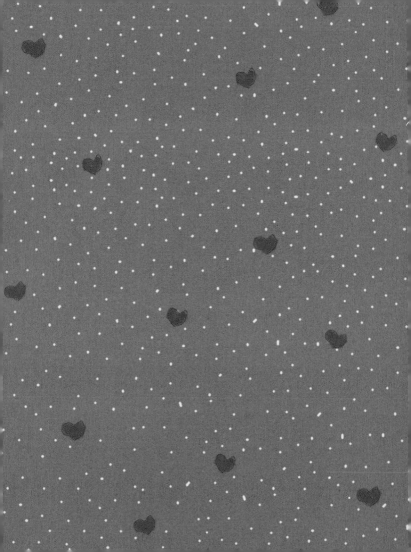